A Time
of Mirrors

D.S. NOONE

ISBN: 1-4392-3055-2
ISBN-13: 9781439230558

Visit www.booksurge.com to order additional copies.

My Love
     The touch of Your hand
          Does still move me
     Your smile
          Can bring me to tears
     The Dawn
          Has held on to its promise
               Of a new day
     As I look into Your eyes
                    Your eyes
          My God   Your eyes
Your lips   enthrall me
     They have held my secrets
          Sung loudly of my accomplishments
          They have been my Siren
               Through this maze of life
                    At times
                         Shattering
                    At times
                         Blissful
                    At all times bearable
               Because of You
                    Only You
                         Know me
                    The darkness
                         The brilliance
                    Only You
                    Would hold me
                         In the sad hours
               Even now
          I give You myself
                         completely

What Love is this
That can
Mist ones eyes
Make one tremble
How can ones breath
Be so labored
In Your presence
Time is lost
Until it brings one closer
My Love
Stay closer
I cannot live without
You

The years
    Have made us one
Our time together
    Has given us memories
        Sunrise and Sunset
            Has shaped You into
                Its finest Creation
As I search
    This Life for Beauty
        It is only You I see
The Beauty of the World
        Is ever changing
    But

            Not You
        Steadfast in Love
                Complete in giving
        We have seen
        Much together
                You and I
The years
    Have made us one

Dance
 Little Dancer
Dance across my Soul
   Fluid
    Alluring
   My Heart is breathless
  Fill Your arms with me
    It is
   Love that guides us
    Dance
      My Dancer
    Dance

In that brief synopsis of time
When the Lush fragrance
Of the moment
Has yet to place its hold
On Your Heart forever
Yet You know
The effect will be
As inevitable as the tides
That brief moment
When Our eyes first met

I could live
     Without the Sun
I could catch Starlight
     And dust the earth
          Before me
          Illuminating
Only that which is Beautiful
     We could walk this road together
          The path being woven
          By moonlight
     Dancing in the eyes
          Of those enamored by Your Soul
     I could walk this life forever
          And never encounter
               Another You

Layers
    Layers of memories
        Beautiful notes
            Played by Loving hands
    To sacrifice for another
        Never given a thought
    Scattered heartaches
        Healed
    Timeless weights
          Given flight
    Her gifted Heart lasts forever
          Life can be
            Hot or cold
        Just pour Yourself
          A moment of Her
           Layers

My faire Angel
    With each breath
        There is a memory
        Each glance
           A mystery
    My desire for You
        Is luminous
           And haunting
    You have
        Reached deep inside me
           And left a Rose
    Through You
        I have seen myself
           In a new light
    With You
        I will gladly spend
                Forever

As You have accomplished Your dreams
With smooth sophistication
You have always maintained
The stature of a dancer
Your excitement
Over the smallest things
Endears me to You
There have been many nights
When my breath
Collided with my heart
As I watched You sleep
When I look at You
Your eyes caress
Past to present
Our time together
The heart that once held You
Holds You still
I would be lost without You

Alas the shadow
Captures light
A talent
Close to madness

And this time
    Paradise will follow
        Four seasons
      And Your smiles
        Will grace many changes
And this time
        All arms will be open
           This time
              Yes this time

Shape me
     Dear palette
A form that is winsome
     With starlit orbs
          That muse insight
     And lips
          Born of enchantment
Pray
Give me the knowledge
     To stop Her from passing
          To other fine ventures
               Far from my presence
     Give me the brush strokes
          To capture
               Her longings
     And keep on my palette
                    My Wife
          My Beloved

From this moment
    The brightest stars
        Will be in Your Lovers eyes
    The most beautiful work of art
           Will be their shining countenance
      They will be
        The alpha of Your existence
    All riches will now pale
        In comparison to Their Smile
      No instrument will move You
        Like the sound of Their voice
  Fill Their chalice
    With Love
      With Trust
        With
  Yourself

In Your
    Well deserved quiet times
        You reflect
            On
    Memories that are etched
        Like the suns cracked visage
            Through aspen trees
        Muted and vaporous
    Yet so strong and distinct nonetheless
            In yearnings past
        Filaments of moonlight
        Portray the intricate dance
            Choreographed by
            The wisdom of Your Heart
        Reflected serenely
    On this finest work of art
        Your Soul

It was a Swan
    That raised me up
        And clothed my back
            And showed me kindness
It was a Swan

Moment to Moment
        The day gets brighter
    Your smile
            More intriguing
    Your breath in slumber
            Becomes my own heartbeat
                Your laugh
            A song I cannot live without
                The child in You
                    Is a vibrant lush echo
            Your sense of commitment
                Has polished my sharp edges
                You
                Have carried me
                    Through many shadows
            Into Your eyes
                I surrender
                A willing captive
    As long as the wind blows
            Through this Life I've been given
                I will Love You
                Moment to Moment

My dearest
    At times
    I am incapable of speech
        To render words to this Passion play
            Unfolding before my eyes
    I may have failed to tell You
            My Elegant Lady
    I have waited all my life
        To breathe You
            To memorize Your eyes
      In this wanting needful world
            I am complete only with You
        Only with You
           Only You

Neither born
 To suits
  Nor jewels
 Life dragged a razor
   Across Your Soul
 But You smiled
   None the less

The mist
A veil of Heavens tears
          Lay akimbo
     Time had washed its hands
          Of a new day   many times
               Still
          He knew rooted in His Heart
               He must fulfill His challenge
                    My God
                    The vigil had been arduous
          Reflecting
               He mused
               How could I have done things better
                    And as that flight of doves had passed
                         Seeing no charred bridges
                              Resolute
                              Inner peace had come
               Still
     The vigil had been arduous

This shell of a man
    Has been filled by You
        With enchantment
    Choreographed
      By Your smile
        That permeates shadows
And is the compass of my desires

Time goes slowly
Until I hear Your voice
My life shallow
Until it breathes You in
I cannot caress Your essence
And it leaves me haunted
An empty vessel am I
And Your laughter fills me
A heart wounded
Touched by a Soul that heals
As wind to sand
It is You who shapes me
The Sun is bright
But You are brilliant
Shine on me
My flawless diamond
Ah
Time goes slowly

Together we could
Knock down the Sun
Split the ocean in half
Put the Wind on the run

The flame You are
      Runs rampant
         Through my Soul
   It casts memories
          Across the walls of time
      Undulating
        Shadow and Spirit
        Past
          And present
Your fire
      Quenches thirst
   Your heat
        Cools the fever
      Your shadow
         Dances brightly
  You are comfort
           In all seasons
This flame You are

She is a seamstress
    Mending Love
        With Her own design
Her artwork
    Defines the beauty
        Of the wearer
    Her fingers
        Touch the fabric
            Of Your Soul
    If Your heart is a patchwork
        She blends the colors
            With the eyes of a genius
        Subtle
            But profound
                She is a seamstress

And maybe
  If we knew Love
New Love
      Would appear

Dawns promise
  Etches rhythmic patterns
    In it's foray
      Across the Room
    Silent in its Overture
        Enigmatic in design
     Such is
       The ragged Wind
         And fugitive Sun

Echo's of a child
    Dance on the wind
        And touch the waves
            That flow towards evening
    Sail on dear Artist
Encounter life's waves
        As only
            You can
    Calm and storm
        Both need to be mastered
    We on the shoreline
            Marvel each moment
        At Your command
            To harness Nature
                And display the Beautiful
    Sail on dear Artist
        As only
            You can

Out of Love
We were given
The gift of sight
Some given more sight
According to their ability
To give Love
Yet
Name one
Who has seen the wind
That undeniable force
So much like
Ones Soul
That has nurtured
Things of Beauty
And given shape
To all we see
The wind is so much like
Ones Soul
I do Love
Your wind through me

At times
I just hear echoes
Blank walls I should embrace
A momentary silence
An abruptly ended chase
I have

Reworded promises
Carbon copied smiles
Hitchhiked to the north end
Wore shoes that
Showed the miles

But
What makes One
A Prophet
A scholar
A healer to us all
In all of life's endeavors
They just stood too tall to fall
Just stood
Too tall
To fall

Black and White
    it all
       Comes down
          to
       Black and White
    Colors
       are for
          the sleight
             of hand
       Me
        I will make
     My final stand
       in
Black and White

I haven't had a chance
To thank You
For those
Brightly colored years
A hand held out
When needed
Gave Love
Instead of tears
A smile
To light the darkness
And Wisdom
For life's road
I haven't had a chance
To thank You
You are
So richly owed

Light and shadow
Compete brilliantly
For the want of Your form
They dance together as no other
They borrow from all beauty
To blend as one
A balance of nature
Second to none
They surrender
Only to You

And in the darkest of nights
　Are there still
　　Clouds in the sky
Has the moon
　Lost its way
　　Is God still breathing

Shed the veils
Reveal the richest tapestry
The most finely milled satin
Ah
Clothes cannot compare
Whether you are rich
With many fine garments
Or poor
With only one
The one who has the most wealth
Is the one
Who finds someone
Who
Can make their body
Feel priceless
And says
Even the mist takes Your form

It appears
            Endless
        Endless
                Endless
Endless
    Endless
Doesn't it

Paint me
Paint me with Your Soul
So often
I have stared
Black fire at the mirror
Blind
To the many colors
You have chosen
Lines You have used
So masterfully
I wished to move
In accordance
To my own dance
In the soirees
With my desires
I have become
Shallow
You see neither color
Nor lines
You see a soul
Paint me

The greatest Lover is
The One who shows
The price of Love
Is never too high
And the gift of themselves
Is the most free of all

Please
Let Her be in my Dreams
While
I am not Dreaming
This time

Simply put
    Just another evening
        Like so many others
           Without You
I spend my time
    Making love to the clock
        Hating every second of it

There is a branch
   On the tree of life
      That has bloomed
           Majestically
  It nurtures
    All it touches
     It has given shade
         In the heat of the moment
       Provided colorful blossoms
             For grey eyes
      And sacrificed all
        To nourish
         The famished
       You have given
         A peace so deep
            One could call it
              Salvation

When the warmth
Of sunlight
Caresses Your face
Does the color of Your skin
Make the feeling different
Does the hue of Your skin
Make the scent of a rose
Any less tantalizing
When You kiss the One You Love
Are You any less breathless
Why place weights
When We are already shackled
Love without bounds   my Friend
Love without bounds

And on this
> Day of Days
Let Us
> > Love
> > and Laugh
> > > and Play
> as if
Tomorrow
> Never happened

What brush is this
    That paints our hours
        Each stroke depicting
            Pleasure or pain
        What pigment is
                Longing or desire
        What hand creates
                These crimsons
                    And deep blues
The inner eye
            That elusive phantom
        Has watched You sweep by
            Never touched to canvas
                Ragged and tallow
                    From the lack of You
                        Brooding and hapless
                            For the want of Your form
    So often each move
            Flowed from self center
        Resulting in grey hues
                And wandering motions
                    The canvas now empty
                Alone in the harsh light
                    Is truly depicting
                        The result of my folly

What's in a moment
      That changes Forever
          A one chance encounter
             That renders You helpless
      To see One whose essence
          Truly heightens Her beauty
            And captures uniquely
               The dreams that have held You
      She has
A smile from which
    You will never recover
And eyes that leave
      A crowded room empty
I will
      Ransom my Heart
         Moment to moment
            For the Love of my life
               Who has changed me
                    Forever

You are a star
    That blazes
        Without competition
    White fire
      From the moon

You have always
      Been a symphony
   Beautifully textured
        Multi layered
Seamlessly You have
   Moved through life
      Leaving melodies
        Exquisite and haunting
          Enriching and timeless
   From silence to crescendo
        You are the music in me

All of our questions
        Are answered in Nature
        From canyon
            To summit
        Solstice
            To moment
    Souls like water
        Reflect their environment
            Tumultuous
                Or placid
            We are the maker
        Thoughts that are sent
                Only true of the sender
            Behold the balance

In every relationship
I was
Looking for a reflection of myself
Just another mask to hide
The face of my fears
We stay together just long enough
Until there is nothing left to steal
Then move on

When You lack
        A fine countenance
    The weight of the world
        Is on the edge
            Of Your smile
        Making it
            Nearly impossible
    To show
            That side
                Of Your Beauty
        The laughter
                Of Your Soul

Whispered notes of Morning
Echo undisturbed
Before the torrent
Of the Day

Here I lie
With my Love
My Desire
My reason for each Heartbeat
She is
My Heart
My Soul
She is
Color in a muted World
She is all I live for
She is
But a Breath away

You are simply
                You
    You have
        Held time captive
            And danced
                With Your heart
            Your vision
                Is one of Love
                To which
                    You have held strong
        Through the eyes
            Of an Angel
                You have seen the valley
                    Through the clouds
            You have walked
                On life's shattered Dreams
                        Barefoot
                    And not cried out
            You have loved
                Beyond words
            You are an oasis
                    To all You encounter
        You are simply
                    You

One's ability
To overcome
One's fear of Life
Is One's ability
To live with Oneself

The man
          Lit a fire on the hills
     Love
          Feeding the flames
     Watching as He approached
               His steps
                    Were sunlight
          I said Father

Together we have shared
  Moonless nights that were Perfect
 You have been
  An inner flame of Rainbows
   For me
  In that slow fall through space
   It has always been
    Only Your hand in mine
  In the landscape of the exquisite
   You are more faire than all others
 In this moment in time
   And forever
   You are my Destiny

The oceans condensed
      To form a single tear
   So pure in its grief
     At the loss of one Soul

We are confused
  Neither aimless nor destructive
    Just confused
  Blind shots
    That missed their mark
   A blend
     Runs through our Hearts
We are confused

You know
        What You do to me
        You have
                Made me walk tall
                        And softened my edges
        You have
                Mesmerized me
                        And given enchantment
                It is for Your form
                        That I search
                                The horizon
                And to my ultimate joy
                                It is me
                                        You come to

                Again
                        And again
                For many years now
                Again
                        And again
        Your beauty has left me
                        Speechless
You know
        What You do to me

Religion is for people
Who want to stay
Out of Hell
Spirituality is for people
Who have seen
Hell

You constantly change
         You constantly change
      You are
                  Constantly Beautiful

After You have gone
        There will still be
            a part of me
    That is not
            Tattered shadows
                and chartless oceans
        I will walk
            Undetected
                Through raw beginnings
        I am here
            where
            it all began
        with the broken edges
            of a
    Well made plan

There has always
　　Been those few
Who choose
　　　To stand alone
　　　　Against all odds
　　To be a guiding light
　　　　A beacon
　　　　　To shelter
What gives them
　　The fortitude
　　I know not
I only know that
　　　Because of You
　　Even in the darkest hour
That Light has always shone on me

I sat by the phone
for so many nights
just waiting
    just waiting for Your call

But the phone
    the phone never once answered
        my prayer

It sat useless
    stunned by the twist of it all

She is so far from me
    not in miles
        but situation

Before Her
    body and Soul could not agree

and my Heart
    my Heart was one beat short
        of a solid sound

Love sought me out
    as far as the Blind can see